I0448094

WHY TOO BIG
TO FAIL?

WHY TOO BIG TO FAIL?

*How the regulatory system
failed the American people.*

KAYE BONNICK

authorHOUSE®

AuthorHouse™
1663 Liberty Drive
Bloomington, IN 47403
www.authorhouse.com
Phone: 1-800-839-8640

© *2010 Kaye Bonnick. All rights reserved.*

No part of this book may be reproduced, stored in a retrieval system, or transmitted by any means without the written permission of the author.

First published by AuthorHouse 1/21/2010

ISBN: 978-1-4490-5437-3 (e)
ISBN: 978-1-4490-5436-6 (sc)

Library of Congress Control Number: 2010900256

Printed in the United States of America
Bloomington, Indiana

This book is printed on acid-free paper.

To my family
Thank you for your love,
encouragement and support.

CONTENTS

FOREWORD

Quis custodiet ipsos custodes? This question was first coined almost four hundred years before the birth of Christ by the exalted Greek philosopher Plato in perhaps his most famous text: *Republic.* Translated from Latin, it means, *"but who will guard the guardians?"*

How profoundly enduring was this perspective that dates back well over twenty centuries. It is particularly resounding when we examine the current debacle within the global financial markets: a viciously engulfing phenomenon that germinated within the so-termed developed countries (led by the United States of America) and rapidly cascaded to the less developed!

What did Plato observe within his own environment that led him to reflect upon a question showing such apprehension and mistrust? Surely, wouldn't it be logical that any person or group that has been granted such crucial and noble responsibilities, to be labeled "guardians" within a society, must have been so appointed by virtue of proven and widely acclaimed credibility? Furthermore, should not the expectation be that these guardians would execute their duties in a just and ethical manner for the benefit of the society that they serve?

Alas, Plato had doubts then, and as we will see in this book—Kaye Bonnick's excellent and enlightening indictment of the modern guardians of the financial markets—we ought to have the same doubts today. Sadly, it appears that rhetoric and reality failed to converge, and we are only left to ask, "Where were our guardians, the government, and why were they not vigilant in protecting the public from potential harm by actions of self-serving corporations?

Despite the well documented recklessness of our major financial services firms and the subsequent disastrous results, the sheer economic size of these institutions has been touted by our guardians as reason for their exemption from the forces of free market dynamics. In other words, they are "too big to fail." Bear in mind, though, that free market dynamics is the very backbone upon which market economics depends to create an optimized world of efficiency and fairness to buyers and sellers alike.

While many have mused over the validity of the notion of "too big to fail," Kaye Bonnick has gone a step beyond, exploring the more pertinent question of why and how these institutions were able to position themselves so strategically in our economy that they have become a sort of untouchable entity, much like a parasite that has penetrated its host so extensively that its demise would also risk the life of the innocent host.

The author begins by rolling back the clock to 1933 to scrutinize important legislative changes that were undertaken during the Depression years to protect the public from potential ruin at the hands of corporations acting irresponsibly in their unbridled pursuit of profit.

She then goes on to reveal a series of questionable reforms in the following decades that not only reversed much of the control and oversight by way of regulatory constraints but went even further to open up new and uncharted opportunities for exploitation by banks and pseudo-banks alike.

As a former investment banker with one of the largest financial services firms, I have read, with great interest, numerous writings on the financial collapse, but I have not seen any that delves into the *why*—the reasons behind the collapse and subsequent government intervention. How did we get to this point of "too big to fail"? If you have been concerned about the state of the financial services industry and you are still not sure how this crisis happened, this book is a must read for you.

So what is the contemporary answer to Plato's question? It ought to be forthcoming once the reader reflects upon the historical record of the government's role in the development of the U.S. financial markets. This account, outlined in lucid detail by the author, shows a consistent pattern of unchecked expansionist policies followed by near-epidemic meltdowns, irreverently termed "market corrections" by "industry experts," and the inevitable toll this phenomenon takes on the lives of ordinary citizens who are far removed from Wall Street and its cadre of lobbyists.

The answer begins with every American citizen. Each must pause long enough to scrutinize the actions of U.S policy makers and regulators. Each must pause long enough to understand the implications of our social and economic planning processes. Most importantly, each must recognize why it is vital to demand the kind of good governance that protects the people, governance that sets rules that simply make good sense and ultimately prevent the country from becoming hostage to the very corporations that would place the nation's stability in peril.

Read on ...
Wayne Spence
Consultant and Former Investment Banker

INTRODUCTION

I first explored the issue of regulation of financial markets in 2001 while pursuing my MBA at Baruch College in New York. It made an interesting study at the time. I had strong opinions then, and I still do now. Much has happened in the past ten years that has significantly affected our financial landscape, and there is still more to come in the aftermath of the most recent collapse.

This book was born from a desire to share my perspective on the financial issues related to the crisis we are facing as a result of the 2008 Wall Street meltdown. Financial issues are sometimes so complicated that the public simply ignores them and hopes for the best. While this crisis is invasive and too widespread to ignore, the issues are still too complicated for many people to understand. Even the "wise" among us are in awe of the developments in the past nine years, since the turn of the twenty-first century.

My objective is to explain some of the key components of the financial meltdown and give readers an understanding of why our government has treated some corporations as "too big to fail." We've heard lots of stories about who said what and who did what on Wall Street and in Washington. That is what I refer to as the "soap opera" sideshow that is interesting and sometimes entertaining—but that does not answer the question of how these events were even possible. How does a private corporation become so big and so important that it cannot be allowed to fail?

There is outrage across our nation because so many individuals are losing their jobs and their homes, yet the government has extended financial assistance to the large corporations at the center of this catastrophe. *Why?* Why did the government commit to a bailout package of approximately $700 billion? The answer lies in financial legislation that was put in place in 1999. This legislation resulted in the creation of financial institutions that were complex and difficult to regulate—but crucial to the health of our financial system.

To assist readers in understanding the nature of our financial framework, I will broadly review the major events of the Great Depression and the financial legislations enacted then to stabilize the financial services industry. I will then discuss the structure of the banking system and how that has evolved over the years through various legislations; provide a look at the critical events during the 1980s with the savings and loan crisis; and explain how we transitioned to the current state of "financial modernization." This historical perspective will provide a foundation for our discussion of the current crisis and of the proposals being offered to prevent a recurrence. The critical question for our country is: do we need to turn back the hands of time or can we move forward with a modernized framework that guards the guardians and the American people?

I will share with you my opinion, which is based on the research I have done, and my hope is that my perspective is helpful.

THE BEGINNING

1929 vs. 2009

On October 24, 1929, the United States stock market suffered a historic crash that has been cited as a contributing cause of the Great Depression. The economic downturn had started earlier, in the summer of 1929, and it escalated with the October stock market crash. The natural response in such a financial crisis was for consumers to stop buying. No one knew what would happen next; consumers responded by ceasing to purchase durable products. The reduction in demand led to a reduction in output—a drop in production—and, ultimately, the Great Depression.[1] The depression did not end until around 1940.

The Depression era was a frightening period for those who lived through it. Banks failed, companies went bankrupt or downsized, unemployment was high, and people feared that they would not be able to provide for their families. Does this sound like the 2008–2009 crisis? Yes, it does. Fortunately, however, we are not experiencing failures of 40 percent of our banks and 20 percent unemployment, as was the case during the Depression era of the 1930s.

How did we climb out of the doldrums of the Great Depression? Did we put in place safeguards to prevent the possibility of widespread collapse in the future? Well, I think we did—and then we undermined our efforts!

Over the years, there have been various theories about the true cause of the Depression, but it cannot be denied that, leading up to that time, banks took serious risks with their depositors' money. Again, there are similarities today, such as the creation of, and investment in, the risky collateralized debt obligations using mortgage-backed securities. Though these particular securities did not exist in the 1930s, risky loans were made and risky investments were both offered and managed through the banks. When these loans failed, so did the banks.

The banking system has experienced many changes since that time, and yet it seems that the industry may have come back to square one. A tenet learned in basic finance courses is that the greater the risk, the higher the return. Well, that's true—but it's also true that the higher the risk, the greater the potential for significant loss. That was true in the 1930s, and it is equally true today. We are in the most severe recession since the Great Depression, and, at this crucial juncture, the way we deal with this crisis will determine our success in the future.

THE GLASS-STEAGALL ACT

In an effort to fix some of the problems that caused the crisis during the Great Depression, Congress enacted the Glass-Steagall Act (GSA) of 1933. The objective of the GSA was to separate commercial and investment banking activities. Commercial banks would no longer be allowed to underwrite or trade corporate stocks or bonds. They would, however, be allowed to purchase and sell Treasury securities and general obligation municipal bonds. On the other hand, investment banks would not be allowed to perform the functions of commercial banks.

Additionally, the GSA restricted commercial banks that were members of the Federal Reserve from affiliating with companies that engaged in investment banking activities. Finally, the GSA also prohibited investment bank directors, officers, employees, or principals from serving in these respective capacities at a member commercial bank. This stipulation was put in place to guard against conflicts of interest.

The GSA also established the Federal Deposit Insurance Corporation (FDIC). The FDIC's role is to insure bank deposits in the event of bank failure. Under the GSA, all member banks of the Federal Reserve had to participate in the FDIC program. The program is similar to a regular insurance policy. The FDIC charges the banks a premium, and, in the event of failure, depositors are guaranteed the return of their money up to the sum insured. The insured value was initially set at $2,500 in 1934; by 1980, the deposit insurance coverage had risen to $100,000. The aim of deposit insurance was to reduce the likelihood of mass withdrawals by depositors, popularly referred to as "a run on the bank."

With the onset of the economic crisis of 2008, the FDIC increased the deposit coverage on interest-bearing accounts to $250,000 and made its coverage unlimited for non-interest-bearing accounts.[2] In the atmosphere of late 2008, amid uncertainty about which bank would collapse next, this temporary measure was intended to reassure citizens that the government would protect our bank deposits. The fears were well founded—there was a run on Wachovia when it became evident that the bank was having difficulties. Wachovia has since been purchased by Wells Fargo.

The GSA also sought to eliminate competition among banks by instituting an interest-rate ceiling for deposits, under Regulation Q. It was determined that interest rate competition among banks contributed to the bank failures of the 1930s. The premise of this regulation was the assumption that, as banks paid high interest rates to attract depositors, they would in turn acquire risky assets—which offered a high rate of return—to bolster their profits. The downside of risky investments is, of course, that the actual return could be lower than expected, which could jeopardize the viability of the commercial banks that hold them. Therefore, as part of the GSA, Congress elected to put an interest rate ceiling of zero on demand deposits (checking accounts) and limit the rates on time and savings deposits (CDs and savings accounts).

In addition to addressing concerns of competition between banks, Regulation Q was geared at encouraging smaller banks to lend their deposits to customers in their immediate communities rather than deposit them with the larger banks. Coming out of the Depression, smaller banks tended to hoard funds instead of making loans, a practice that delays economic recovery and growth. This practice is based on fear about the overall economic recovery, but it creates a vicious cycle. An economy needs active lending to stimulate growth, but financial institutions are crippled by the fear that the economy will not grow—the resulting credit freeze, in effect, causes that fear to become reality. Without lending, the economy does not grow.

Despite the apparent success of the Glass-Steagall Act, there were those who held a dissenting view. It has even been said that, two years after its enactment, one of its sponsors, Senator Carter Glass, said that he thought it had been a mistake and an overreaction and that he wanted to amend the act. However, in light of the 2008 crisis, it could be argued that the GSA may have had some redeeming qualities.

THE FINANCIAL SERVICES SYSTEM

COMPONENTS OF THE FINANCIAL SERVICES INDUSTRY

The financial services industry includes several different types of institutions that serve different needs: depository institutions, insurance companies, investment banks, finance companies, mutual funds, and hedge funds. Our focus will be on the depository institutions and investment banks.

The diagram shows the basic flow of money between consumers and some financial intermediaries. Rather than keep their money in cookie jars, individuals want to have a safe place to save—and earn interest on—their money. These intermediaries, which can be commercial banks, savings and loan associations, credit unions, or other types of institutions, accept deposits from individuals and hold the money in various types of accounts (savings, checking, etc.). These intermediaries use their customers' deposits to provide loans to other customers. The borrowers may be depositors themselves, but oftentimes they are not.

Loans, which might be intended for personal or commercial use, are usually needed for large purchases such as cars and homes, or to start or expand a business.

The overriding expectation in this system is that loans are made at a higher interest rate than that paid to the depositors; the difference is a net gain to the institution.

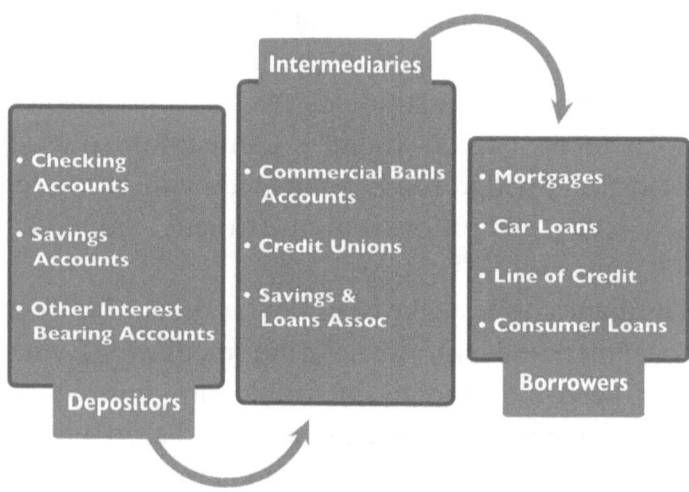

Financial intermediaries take advantage of modern technology to easily conduct business globally. Electronic fund transfers, online bill payments, wire transfers, and other automated financial transactions have accelerated the pace at which business is conducted and, in some instances, have shattered barriers that made trade inconvenient.

Our banking system is at the center of the growth of the American economy, and, not surprisingly, it is at the center of our current crisis. Though the banks are the main focus of scrutiny, they are not the sole perpetrators of the current financial tsunami. The economic crisis of 2008–2009 is a complex problem with many places to lay blame.

Within the financial framework, one element of concern is the insufficient level of capital reserves held by failing institutions. To start and maintain a business, capital is required. A financial intermediary is no different from any other business; however, their capital requirements are determined by their charting agency. Typically, a financial institution is required to have a certain ratio of capital to assets.

Assets for a bank are generally the loans made to customers that are outstanding and the investments kept on its balance sheet. In the event that borrowers default on their loans or the value of an institution's investments declines sharply, the institution should have sufficient capital reserves (cash) to continue doing business despite the losses incurred.

Internationally, capital requirements are set by the Basel Committee. In early 2009, as a response to the global financial crisis, the Basel II framework was strengthened to ensure greater capital requirements. Most, if not all, large financial intermediaries and investment firms have international divisions. Following the principle that "a chain is only as strong as its weakest link," international regulatory mechanisms, such as the Basel Committee, were compelled to act to ensure that financial institutions would take steps to safeguard the interests of their depositors and investors.

Investment banks, unlike commercial banks, do not provide what is called "cash management services." That is, they do not provide traditional checking and savings accounts or any of the other services mentioned previously. Investment banks underwrite and trade securities. The term *securities* includes many other products besides the familiar stocks and bonds, such as swaps, options, futures, swap-options (swaptions), and asset-backed securities. These are called derivatives.

The underwriting role of the investment bank involves advising a company interested in issuing stocks or bonds on what price they could ask for their offering, applying to the Securities and Exchange Commission (SEC) for permission to offer the security, and preparing and distributing the prospectus, which provides all the details about the company and the intended security sale. The investment bank can handle the offer in one of two ways: a "firm commitment" or a "best-efforts" agreement.

Under a firm commitment, an investment firm would purchase the entire offering from the issuing company, and that firm would, in turn, sell the security to the public. In such a scenario, the risk is transferred to the investment company. For example, if the public does not see the issuing company in a favorable light, there would be less demand for the company's security. This would drive down the price of the security, and the investment company would lose money on that deal.

Therefore, the more popular approach is the best efforts agreement, where the investment bank helps the issuing company to sell its security, but the investment bank does not actually purchase the security. Once a security has been sold, it becomes available to be traded on an exchange. At this point, brokerage houses and online discount brokers enter the picture. On behalf of investors, these brokerage firms trade on exchanges such as the New York Stock Exchange (NYSE) or on the over-the-counter markets, such as the National Association of Securities Dealers Automated Quotation System (NASDAQ).

Many investment firms, such as Bear Stearns and Lehman Brothers, were "super companies" that did it all. They engaged in underwriting, advising, and securities trading. However, despite their size and wealth, the mortgage crisis brought these giants to their knees.

The Federal Reserve System

In 1913, the Federal Reserve was created. The "Fed," as it is commonly called, is the central banking system of the United States. One of its main roles is to ensure that the credit system remains stable and functional. To this end, the Fed regulates the banks that are members of the Federal Reserve.

Banks can have either a national or a state charter. When the Fed was established, nationally chartered banks were obligated to be members, while state-chartered banks had the option of being members. Once they joined the Federal Reserve System, banks were required to hold a reserve of funds to meet short-term demands, called the reserve requirement. The amount of required reserves was based on their level of deposits and was separate from their capital requirement.

A benefit of being a member bank is that members can borrow from the Fed and from each other.

However, the Fed restricted the types of assets that member banks could hold.

The Federal Reserve System is governed by a seven-member Board of Governors. The members of the board are appointed by the president of the United States and are subject to Senate confirmation.

The Federal Reserve is responsible for setting the federal funds target rate, the discount rate, and the reserve requirements, mentioned above. We have heard many times that the Fed may change interest rates, and we often wait with great expectancy to see what the Fed will do. The rate set by the Fed is the *target* federal funds rate, and the financial markets react whenever a change is announced. Through interbank negotiations, as borrowing takes place, the *effective* federal funds rate is determined.

The federal funds rate is the rate at which banks can borrow from each other's excess reserves. Through the interbank funding process, banks lend to each other to cover their reserve requirements on a short-term basis, usually overnight. On the other hand, the *discount* rate is the rate at which banks can borrow from the discount window at the Federal Reserve.

If the Fed lowers interest rates, the following may happen:

1.   Banks will be able to access money at a lower rate and will be more willing to give loans to consumers.

2.   Mortgage rates *might* be lowered, and therefore more consumers might consider purchasing homes. Mortgage rates do not respond directly to changes in the discount rate, but if the discount

rate is kept low for a significant period of time, this could eventually lead to lower mortgage rates.

3.   Commercial interest rates may be lowered, which would encourage major capital purchases by businesses. Expansion of businesses and increased investments in more efficient processes are the anticipated outcomes of reduced commercial rates.

Therefore, lowering interest rates can stimulate credit markets and the economy. This is a monetary control tool used by the Federal Reserve Bank to guide the direction of the economy. Banks play a crucial role in the execution of this process.

POST-DEPRESSION RECOVERY

Over the years, more and more banking regulations were instituted to guard against widespread failures. The 1950s marked the beginning of an era when financial services institutions sought ways to expand their business and circumvent the various regulations.

Banks felt that the existing regulations hindered their competitive ability and limited their growth.

As banks looked for loopholes, they began to form corporate shells called Bank Holding Companies (BHCs) to own both banking and non-banking businesses. These corporate shells would acquire multiple banks and were referred to as "multi-bank holding companies."

In response, Congress enacted the Bank Holding Act of 1956, which prohibited BHCs from acquiring banks in other states. In a subsequent amendment to this law, BHCs became subject to the state laws of the state where they wished to acquire a bank. If that state allowed for a national bank to acquire and operate a bank locally, then the BHC was free to do so. However, most states did not allow this, and, essentially, BHCs were prohibited from operating banks across state lines. The Bank Holding Act also restricted the ability of bank holding companies to engage in most non-banking activities or to acquire voting securities in companies that were not banks.

The Bank Holding Act was one of several laws enacted to regulate, and to some extent limit, banking activities. The McFadden Act, in 1927, had been instituted to restrict bank branching across state lines. The purpose of this act was to provide states with the ability to govern national banks that sought branches in their state. If banks were allowed to operate subsidiary banks in other states, regulators feared creation of large organizations, too much risk, and a competitive environment.

So, what's wrong with competition?

Well, competition creates *greed,* and greed leads to risky behavior and risky behavior … well, we see the results in the financial meltdown in 2008. The Bank Holding Act would have worked fairly well except for a provision in section 4c of the act. This loophole stated that the Federal Reserve could allow BHCs to engage in activities that the Board determined to be "closely related to banking or managing or controlling banks as to be a proper incident thereto."[3]

What this meant was, if a BHC wanted to acquire control of a non-bank, it had to get the approval of the Federal Reserve. Before granting approval, the Federal Reserve Board administered a two-part test. First, they determined whether the non-bank activity was "closely related to banking or managing or controlling banks," and then they performed a public benefits test to determine whether the activity was a "proper incident thereto." The results of these tests would determine whether or not permission was granted to the BHC to acquire a non-bank entity and therefore to engage in non-banking activities.

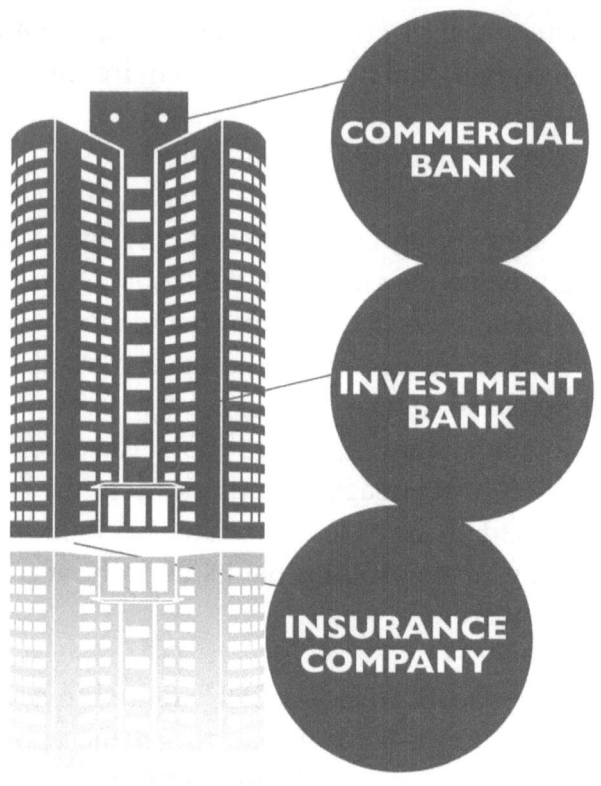

However, the Bank Holding Act regulated only multibank holding companies that, as the name suggests, had more than one bank in their corporate structure. The Bank Holding Act did not apply to One-Bank Holding Companies (OBHCs). Financial institutions exploited this avenue to engage in non-banking activities and interstate banking. In

1970, the Bank Holding Act was amended to bring OBHCs under the same regulation.

Evidently, there was an ongoing struggle between the banks and the Fed. The banks constantly pushed the limits to legally expand their business, while the Federal Reserve tried to use regulations to keep them in check. Unfortunately, I would say, there are always the proverbial loopholes that provide opportunities to challenge the law and the status quo. It is likely that our partisan political process contributes to these weaknesses in our legislation.

In addition to the loopholes that existed, non-member banks were free to legally affiliate with securities firms. That's right; despite the GSA it was still possible for these entities to offer a wider range of products than the member commercial banks that were regulated by the act. Therefore, the law was applied unevenly to essentially similar institutions. Furthermore, securities brokers' cash management accounts, which function like a checking account, were not recognized as deposits and were therefore not subject to the restrictions of depository institutions.

As inflation increased, the federal interest rate ceilings, created by Regulation Q, began to affect the ability of banks to attract deposits. They could not attract sufficient deposits to meet loan demand at Regulation Q rates. As mentioned earlier, the regulation, which was part of the Glass-Steagall Act, put a ceiling on the interest rates that could be offered by banks to their depositors. This ceiling was an effort to create a fair playing field by limiting banks' ability to compete by offering unfairly high returns for deposits. However, consumers began to find alternative high-yielding vehicles in which to invest their money.

Banks were losing money to investment institutions that were not subject to the same restrictions as they were. With deposits shrinking, the banks' ability to create loans was also shrinking, which affected their profits. When funds are withdrawn from traditional depository institutions, such as commercial banks and savings and loan associations, to be put directly into investment firms, the process is called "disintermediation."

DISINTERMEDIATION AND THE SAVINGS AND LOAN CRISIS

Depositors tipped the scale in favor of investment and securities firms because of the variety of choices and higher yielding products available to them.

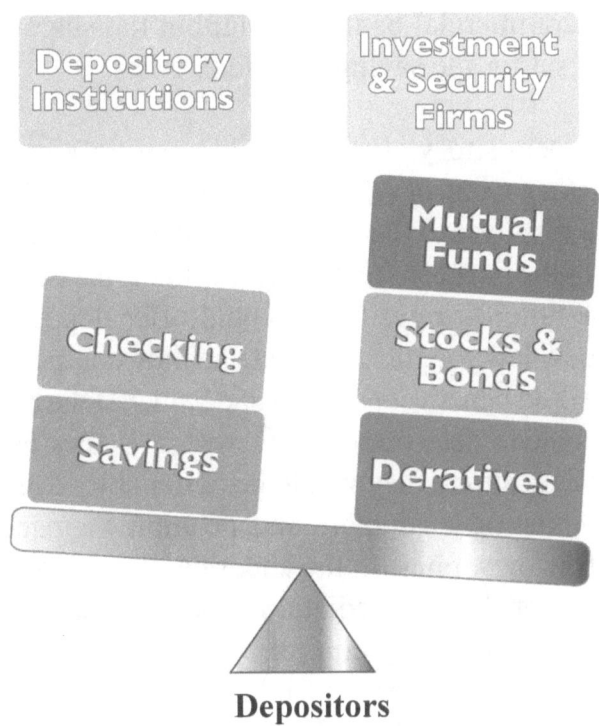

Depositors

However, as I mentioned earlier, banks kept pushing to do more. Of course, the banks found a way to challenge the interest rate restrictions—they developed money market accounts and Negotiable Order of Withdrawal (NOW) accounts. Money market deposit accounts are used as an investment vehicle to offer depositors a higher rate of return on their "deposit," while allowing them access to these funds on demand, as they could with a checking account. On the other hand, NOW accounts are simply interest-bearing accounts against which checks can be drawn. However, by 1980, not only were commercial banks failing, but the stage was being set for the savings and loan crisis.

The Depository Institution Deregulation and Monetary Control Act (DIDMCA), passed in 1980, was a response to the problem of disintermediation. One of the purposes of this act was to lift the ceilings on the interest rates banks could offer depositors. The new law sought to promote healthy competition that would benefit consumers and banks. If the banks were able to determine the interest rates they could offer depositors, they would be better able to retain their existing customers and position themselves to attract new ones. In the end, this would slow the process of disintermediation. The act also sought to tighten monetary control by extending Federal Reserve requirements to both member and non-member banks and also to savings and loan banks, also called thrift institutions or thrifts. Commercial banks now had the inroad they needed to become more competitive, but the act might have been the downfall of the savings and loan banks.

Savings and loan banks were typically small institutions that mainly offered savings accounts and residential mortgage loans to their members. As outlined in the FDIC study on the savings and loan industry, titled *History of the Eighties – Lessons for the Future*,[4] a federally chartered stock association had the following guidelines:

- It was required to have a minimum of 400 stockholders.

- No individual could own more than 10 percent of the firm's outstanding stock.

- No controlling group could have more than 25 percent of the institution's outstanding stock.

- 75 percent of stockholders had to reside or do business in the savings and loan's market area.

These guidelines give us a sense of what type of organizations savings and loan banks were at that time—small and community focused. Prior to DIDMCA, they operated in an inflationary environment with high interest rates and were subject to the Regulation Q restrictions. The savings and loan banks were struggling to stay in operation.

With the DIDMCA, the following regulatory changes were made:[5]

- The net worth requirement for thrifts changed from 5 percent to a range of 3 percent to 6 percent of insured accounts, but the exact percentage would be determined by the Federal Home Loan Bank Board (FHLBB).

- Savings and loan banks could offer a wider variety of depository products and at higher rates than they would have been able to before.

- Thrifts would be allowed to make ADC Loans—acquisition, development, and construction loans.

- The FDIC insurance coverage increased to $100,000.

Despite these regulatory changes, designed to help the Thrifts grow out of their problems, between 1980 and 1982, 118 savings and loan banks failed. In response to the continued problems in the industry, the Garn-St. Germain Depository Institutions Act (GSGDIA) of 1982 was passed. The main purpose of the act was to further deregulate thrifts; in so doing, it loosened the capital requirements for thrifts and determined that the Federal Savings and Loan Insurance Corporation (FSLIC) would determine those new, relaxed requirements. This act also allowed for adjustable rate mortgages, in an effort to encourage home ownership. Adjustable rate mortgages (ARMs) are a centerpiece in the current foreclosure crisis.

Both the DIDMCA and the GSGDIA deregulated the savings and loan bank industry in an attempt to save struggling institutions. The objective was for the FSLIC to avoid having to close banks and pay out on insured deposits. However, this deregulated environment pushed the thrifts into risky activities, such as 100 percent funding for real estate development projects and paying high interest rates to remain competitive.

Unfortunately, the management of these savings and loan banks had little experience with these products and was not able to manage them well. The savings and loan banks began to offer a larger number of consumer loans and risky mortgages, which left them very exposed and poised to fail.

Many of the risky mortgages were speculative investments. When the real estate tax laws changed in 1986, with the Tax Reform Act, property owners started to dump these properties because they no longer provided a tax shelter. Therefore, market prices fell, and the number of mortgage defaults increased. In addition, the government had relaxed its oversight of the industry, giving the thrifts less-stringent guidelines for their financial reporting, and it had removed the requirement for a minimum number of members in these institutions. Taken together, these events proved to be a cocktail for disaster.

During this dynamic period, along with the many changes taking place in the operational management of these institutions, the economy was suffering from high inflation. The Fed battled inflation by increasing the interest rate; therefore the cost of funding increased (as explained under the Federal Reserve section). The interest payments that banks were receiving from their borrowers were mainly fixed, though, and therefore their profit was dwindling. The combination of lower profits and failing loans meant that there was not much hope for recovery for many of the thrift institutions. The Federal Savings and Loan Insurance Corporation (FSLIC) went bankrupt as a result of having to guarantee the deposits of the customers of so many failed savings and loan banks. However, prior to its insolvency, the FSLIC was authorized to borrow more than $10 billion from the government. Therefore, the taxpayers were a part of the bailout that occurred in the thrift industry twenty years ago.

As a result of continued failures in the financial industry, Congress passed the Financial Institutions Reform, Recovery, and Enforcement Act (FIRREA) of 1989. The purpose of the FIRREA was to provide the funding necessary to resolve failed, and failing, savings and loan banks, and to put safeguards in place to reduce the possibility of such a crisis in the future. The FIRREA made the following fundamental changes to the regulatory landscape of the thrift industry:[6]

1. The Federal Home Loan Bank Board and the Federal Savings and Loan Insurance Corporation were eliminated.

2. The Resolution Trust Corporation (RTC) was established to liquidate failing thrifts.

3. The Office of Thrift Supervision (OTS) was created to replace the FHLBB.

4. Two new insurance funds were created: the Savings Association Insurance Fund (SAIF) and the Bank Insurance Fund (BIF). Both came under the supervision on the FDIC.

5. Capital requirements were increased.

6. Thrifts would not be allowed to buy and hold low-grade junk bonds unless they were held in a subsidiary with a separate capital base.

7. Stricter regulations were put in place regarding the percentage of a thrift's

assets that could be held as consumer and business loans.

8. Banks and thrifts were required to pay increased insurance premiums to the insurance fund.

9. Banks were allowed to buy thrifts that were failing.

In summary, the government deregulated the thrift industry to give savings and loan banks room to take greater risks with the objective of earning greater returns to stabilize the banks. When that was not successful, the government embarked on a path of re-regulation with the FIRREA. In the end, more than fifteen hundred thrifts had failed during this crisis. The cost to taxpayers of the savings and loan crisis has been estimated to be $132 billion.[7]

BANKS VS. THE FEDERAL RESERVE

The 1980s saw the change from "relationship" banking to "transactional" banking.[8] Previously, banks had depended heavily on established relationships with customers as the basis for their lending business. As banks tried to expand their business and to attract new customers, they had to move away from that model and do business with clients with whom they did not necessarily have a relationship. Banks began to offer cash management services and computerized programs that allowed account holders to readily access information about their bank accounts and transfer balances and funds.

Banks continued to increase their role in providing financial services. This included selling stocks and bonds, providing advice on mergers and acquisitions, and developing new financial products and services.[9] As banks continued to infringe on the securities market, the existing financial laws were used to slow the process. However, while the Supreme Court made rulings that upheld some provisions of the Glass-Steagall Act, bank regulators recognized that banks needed to expand their business models to survive, and they continued to pave the way for banks to expand their securities business.

Section 20 of the GSA, which prohibited commercial banks from affiliating with investments firms, came under increasing attack from the banks. In *Securities Industry Association v. Board of Governors of the Federal Reserve System*, the District of Columbia Circuit Court of Appeals held that the Fed could allow bank affiliates to engage in up to 5 percent of ineligible securities activities without violating the GSA restriction. The restriction, of course, was that bank affiliates should not be "principally engaged" in such activity.

Banks have been defined as financial institutions that offer both demand deposits and commercial loans. Both of these criteria must be met for an institution to be legally defined as a bank and therefore subject to the regulations of bank regulatory agencies. BHCs used this loophole to develop firms that could bypass banking regulations. In response, Congress passed the Competitive Equality Banking Act of 1987, which imposed a one-year moratorium on Federal Reserve approval of further securities activities by banks. A bank was then redefined as an institution that has FDIC insurance or that both accepts deposits and makes commercial loans.

In summary, several issues raised in the late 1980s related to banks and the Federal Reserve. A key issue was the restrictions on Federal Reserve member banks that barred them from entering the investment banking industry, putting them at a competitive disadvantage with other financial institutions. In 1988, bank failures reached a post-Depression record, and, for the first time, the FDIC sustained a loss and continued to have losses until 1991. Nevertheless, the banks continued their aggressive fight against the prevailing regulatory system in their quest to become competitive and profitable.

CITIBANK AND J. P. MORGAN: THEIR ROLE IN THE FALL OF THE GSA

J. P. Morgan & Co. had to split when the Glass-Steagall Act became law. Morgan Stanley focused on investment banking, and J. P. Morgan stuck with the lending business. J.P Morgan was at the forefront of the fight to break through the firewall erected by the GSA between investment and retail banking. In 1989, the Federal Reserve gave J. P. Morgan permission to underwrite corporate debt securities, and in 1990, the company was permitted to sell stock through a subsidiary, although the stock market operations had to be limited to 10 percent of the company's revenues. With the experience they had gained in Europe, J. P. Morgan was ready to make waves in the U.S financial markets. This waiver was one of the official darts thrown at the GSA by the Federal Reserve, culminating in its eventual repeal.

In 1990, Citibank challenged the Federal Reserve's interpretation of section 20 of the GSA. The Fed's interpretation of section 20 could have differing impacts on the section 20 subsidiaries, depending on the product that they offered. Citibank advocated for multiple revenue limits based on different products. As mentioned earlier, the limit was set at 10 percent at that time.

The Fed argued that multiple standards would create substantial uncertainty among section 20 subsidiaries and the potential for inconsistent interpretations of the statue among the subsidiaries as well as the examiners.[10]

Even so, the Fed announced in December 1996 that it was increasing from 10 percent to 25 percent the amount of total revenues that a non-bank subsidiary of a bank holding company could derive from underwriting and dealing in securities. The Fed justified this decision, six years after Citibank's initial request, on the basis that their experience since 1987 had shown them that the 10 percent limit unduly restricted the underwriting and dealing activity of the section 20 subsidiaries. This allowed banks to expand their securities business even further in their section 20 affiliates without violating the Glass-Steagall Act.

These allowances paved the way for regulatory overhaul on the eve of the twenty-first century. The Glass-Steagall Act was going up in smoke. *Out with the old and in with the new ...*

Financial modernization was about to be unleashed!

Financial Modernization for the Twenty-First Century

THE FINANCIAL
MODERNIZATION ACT

The Gramm-Leach-Bliley Act (GLBA), which was signed into law on November 12, 1999, modified the existing federal banking law. This law is also known as the Financial Modernization Act.

THE GLBA VS. THE GSA

The GLBA repeals the Glass-Steagall prohibition of affiliation between Federal member banks and entities involved in securities activities. It also repealed the prohibition of officials of securities entities serving in supervisory positions in member banks.[11] In essence, the GLBA repeals sections 20 and 32 of the GSA.

The new law promotes consolidations within the financial services industry by allowing new Financial Holding Companies (FHCs) to own subsidiary corporations involved in any activity that is financial in nature. However, the act was designed to protect against the negative effects of this kind of consolidation: a bank holding company seeking FHC status must be "well capitalized" and "well managed" at a minimum. In addition to this, the BHC must pass the minimum requirements of the Community Reinvestment Act (CRA). The CRA was enacted in 1977 to encourage banks to lend within their local communities, including low- to middle-income areas. A record of banks' performance is kept to evaluate how well they are supporting the local community.

The GLBA restricts cross-marketing arrangements within FHCs between the bank and its non-financial subsidiaries, and the act requires reports on the impact of the financial modernization on small businesses and farms. The scope of activities permitted to FHCs is intended to be broader than that permitted to BHCs under the Bank Holding Company Act. The Gramm-Leach-Bliley Act redefines some previously impermissible activities as "financial in nature" and allows FHCs to engage in these activities without prior notice to the Federal Reserve Board.[12] These include:

- Underwriting or dealing in securities without revenue or position limitations;
- Organizing, sponsoring, or distributing a mutual fund;

- Making merchant banking investment in companies, regardless of the activities in which the companies are engaged, if the investment activity is conducted through a securities or insurance affiliate or another appropriate non-bank affiliate;
- Underwriting insurance and issuing annuities;
- Selling insurance as agent or broker; and
- Engaging, within the United States, in any activity that has previously been permissible abroad under the Federal Reserve Board's Regulation K or under interpretations of the Federal Reserve Act and the International Banking Act, such as travel agency, real estate brokerage, or management consulting.

Further, the GLBA protects the privacy of customers. Regulatory agencies must establish standards to protect the confidentiality and integrity of customer information. Generally, institutions are not allowed to disclose private account information to unaffiliated third parties. Finally, the act requires that banks that operate automatic teller machines (ATMs) must post notice of any fees charged for the use of the ATMs and must provide notice of fees upon issuance of an ATM card.

The GLBA also amends the Bank Holding Company Act by requiring the Fed to notify the Federal Trade Commission (FTC) of any merger or acquisition involving non-banking interests, and it expands the categories of mergers and acquisitions that must be reported to the FTC pursuant to the Hart-Scott-Rodino Act.[13]

A key feature of the new financial services legislation is a shift toward functional regulation of financial institutions.[14] Prior to the enactment of the GLBA, financial institutions were regulated along industry lines, using an "entity" focused approach: The Office of the Comptroller of the Currency (OCC) regulated national banks. The Federal Reserve regulated state banks that were members of the Federal Reserve System and regulated bank holding companies. State regulators, along with the Federal Deposit Insurance Corporation (FDIC), regulated state banks that were not Federal Reserve members. The Securities and Exchange Commission (SEC) and the National Association of Securities Dealers regulated broker-dealer firms. State insurance commissioners regulated insurance companies.

The Financial Modernization Act changed the way authority was allocated among these regulators. Under the new system, regulatory authority is allocated on the basis of the *nature of the activity being performed,* rather than being allocated based on the institutional identity of the firm conducting the activity. The Federal Reserve Board is, however, the "umbrella" regulatory body that is supposed to ensure the overall soundness of an institution. Interestingly, the passage of the Gramm-Leach-Bliley Act can be traced directly to the Federal Reserve's liberal interpretation of section 20 of the Glass-Steagall Act.

It is often said that hindsight is 20/20: While the GLBA authorized several different regulators per firm, it created a fractured approach to regulation that was relatively ineffective.

The GLBA was expected to provide greater convenience for customers, expansion of available services, and lower fees, *but it did much more*.

TRAVELERS-CITICORP MERGER: THE FINAL PUSH

In 1998, the Federal Reserve Board had permitted Citicorp, one of the largest BHCs in the United States, to become affiliated with Travelers Group, a diversified financial services firm engaged in insurance and securities activities. The value of this merger was $83 billion. The combined entity had more than one hundred million customers worldwide, and it offered a wide range of products that varied from corporate finance to consumer banking and securities. This merger essentially pushed the enactment of the Gramm-Leach-Bliley Act in the following year.

ISSUES AND CONSEQUENCES

The merger and passage of the GLBA raised the following concerns and led to the following consequences:

- Prior to the passage of the GLBA, the newly merged Citicorp/Travelers institution would have had to divest its insurance underwriting business within five years. Opponents of the merger suspected that the company had never intended to divest, but rather, it had intended all along to force the law to change. The powerful conglomerate succeeded—creating the opportunity for the development of other financial "superpowers."

- There was concern that this historic merger, that helped to push the repeal of the GSA, would lead to a wave of mergers within the financial services industry. The greatest fear was that there would be growth in huge corporations, those considered "too big to fail." The pressure on the Federal Reserve Board to ensure that these institutions did not fail could have a far-reaching impact on the future of the financial industry. The question at that time was whether we would be faced with another collapse in the banking industry in the future similar to the crisis that had led to enactment of the Glass-Steagall Act.

- Another pressing issue was the question of regulating these financial "supermarkets." The GLBA had instituted functional regulation. With the possibility of an impending wave of mergers, the Federal Reserve would be challenged to ensure that the institutions were being regulated properly. Within a large conglomerate such as Citigroup, conducting many types of financial activities, how would functional regulation guarantee that all aspects of its business would be regulated properly? Would the Federal Reserve be able to monitor these large institutions closely enough to prevent ill effects?

- With the Federal Reserve serving as the umbrella agency for regulating the financial services industry, competition should have been reduced among the OCC, FDIC, the Federal Reserve, and other regulatory bodies. However, since the Federal Reserve was no longer required to compete for regulatory turf with other agencies, its incentive to innovate and adjust to competitive concerns could diminish. The concern was particularly acute in light of the argument that "the Fed has a history of suppressing innovation, very conservative management, and a readiness to take broad requests from Congress for restricting new activities."[15] What then would be the true benefit to the consumers of large institutions with vast resources, yet whose ability to innovate was suppressed?

- Consumer advocates worried that consumers' privacy would be compromised. Though the law protected against the sharing of information, the burden was with consumers to opt out of information sharing among the institution's affiliates. If a consumer did not actively opt for privacy, all their personal information would be available to all members of the conglomerate. For example, if a consumer was affiliated with a bank and an insurance company individually, and then they merged, that consumer's combined information would be accessible to both parties.

- Anticompetitive market powers could develop from large mergers. Citigroup, with its vast reach, was actually in a position to raise prices on some of its financial products without losing clients because it could offer the convenience of one-stop shopping. With the potential for more mergers in the future, would consumers find themselves paying more for services?

- Major consolidations, such as the Citicorp-Travelers merger, could lead to anticompetitive effects in smaller regions. Small-scale regional or local financial institutions would find it extremely difficult to compete with large conglomerates, and they could also become the targets of acquisitions.

- Small businesses could find it more difficult to get loans from the newly formed financial institutions, as their creditworthiness might come under closer scrutiny. Small businesses might formerly have obtained loans from their local banks based on their "presence" in the community and the understanding that they would honor their obligations. Large national conglomerates would not have the intimate knowledge of small businesses, and the potential impact on the community could be considered negligible and unimportant.

- As more companies merged, shareholders of the target companies would experience a boost in their share value, while the acquiring firm's shareholders would lose value. The premise is that an acquiring firm is willing to pay premium prices for the shares of their target in order to make the acquisition—their shareholders pay the price. While there are laws to discourage insider trading, multiple mergers create temptation, fueling fears of an increase in this illegal activity.

- Sponsors of the GLBA did consider the possibility of anticompetitive effects. Title I of the act gives authority to the justice department, along with the Federal Trade Commission, to conduct the necessary anti-trust review for new financial combinations allowed under the act. In all fairness, it must be acknowledged that the GLBA considered the potential negative effects of large and "threatening" mergers like the Citicorp-Travelers merger. The GLBA grants authority to different regulatory bodies to examine issues prior to the approval of mergers. However, it's possible that, as in the Glass-Steagall Act, loopholes will be found in the Gramm-Leach-Bliley Act.

"It may be just a matter of time before we see the true effect of this new legislation and what it brings in its wake."

I said that eight years ago. It is striking that we are now experiencing the consequences of the issues I was concerned about then. Let's take a look at life in the financial industry since the Gramm-Leach-Bliley Act.

THE UNRAVELING

The Current Crisis: 2008–2009

We've been bombarded by reports in the media about the scary state of our economy, but even more than that, we've been feeling and seeing firsthand the true state of our economy. We see our friends and family being laid off from their jobs and manufacturing companies closing their doors because they can't compete with cheaper imports or they can't get the credit or loans that they need to continue operations; we see the price of gas inching up once again; and we hold our breaths, hoping that today will not be the day that we are the ones to get the pink slip.

This crisis, which started in 2007, has been described as the worst economic downturn since the Great Depression. In that, really, lies the answer to why these companies are "too big to fail". Having another Great Depression is not an option. Certain corporations are so huge and complex that they are literally holding the country for ransom, and we have no choice but to meet their demands.

Some say that the start of this crisis was the mortgage mess—rising rates of foreclosures and the corresponding fall in property values. While I do agree that this was the pin that burst the bubble, I dare argue that the crisis started earlier—when we allowed these financial superpowers to develop. Compounding the problem was our inability to ensure that they were properly regulated once we allowed them to form.

Additionally, we saw the development of creative financial products, which appeared to be, or were presented as, low risk, but, in fact, turned out to be some of the most risky investment products ever: mortgage-backed securities (MBSs), collateralized debt obligations (CDOs) and credit default swaps (CDSs). To understand how mortgage-backed securities were developed, it is important to understand what was happening in the mortgage industry. We'll also see how these financial instruments fit into the subprime mortgage market.

In the early eighties, there was a housing crisis—real estate values had fallen, and new legislation was passed, intended to stimulate growth in the financial industry and the mortgage industry; the savings and loan crisis was eminent. Some of the new legislation permitted banks to offer adjustable rate mortgages (ARMs), a new twist in real estate financing. In place of a traditional 15- or 30-year fixed mortgage, an ARM allows the mortgage holder a low initial interest rate that, at some point during the repayment period, adjusts to a higher rate. The terms of the ARM are set at the time the loan is granted. An ARM might involve more than one rate adjustment, and the future rates are not fixed or known. The interest rate of the mortgage will change as the base interest rate, such as the prime rate, changes. However, most ARMs have a cap on how much the rate is allowed to increase in a given year.

There is an additional factor. Have you received notice that your mortgage had been sold to an entity other than the bank where you took out the mortgage? There is a market for selling mortgages. The purchasing institutions take over the risk of the loans; the original mortgage lender has been repaid for those loans. This is called the secondary mortgage market. After selling mortgages, the original lender has the resources to lend again, and the cycle continues.

An additional major change in the mortgage industry was the introduction of subprime lending. Essentially, loans were made to individuals who were not qualified for the loans. Perhaps you've seen media stories on people who were going through foreclosure proceedings. Maybe they were earning $50,000 per year, and they had a mortgage for $500,000. That may be a slight exaggeration, but that would be an example of subprime, predatory lending: loans that cannot be supported by the income of the borrower. Why would people put themselves in this situation? Usually, they just wanted to live the American dream. In the end, however, many simply created hardships for themselves in pursuit of their dreams.

With a strong desire to build wealth, lured by the promise of a mortgage they could "afford," and with financial institutions providing the vehicle to do so, a tremendous number of people jumped at the opportunity to buy their dream house.

A better question to ask is, why did financial institutions buy these mortgages and take on that risk? To make money of course! Wall Street firms bought the risky mortgages and created new financial products, which they then sold to investors. This practice started with Fannie Mae and Freddie Mac and then spread to other financial services firms. Fannie and Freddie are publicly traded companies with a profit motive.

Another question to ask is, should the mortgage lenders have been able to offer such risky loans? Any rational person will say no! So how was it possible?

FANNIE, FREDDIE, AND GINNIE MAE

The government places a priority on encouraging home ownership. Two government sponsored entities (GSEs), Fannie Mae (Federal National Mortgage Association) and Freddie Mac (Federal Home Loan Mortgage Corporation), played an important role in that process. They are privately owned institutions, chartered by Congress, meaning they are not government agencies, but they have the "aura" that the government guarantees their financial stability. Their role was to expand lending to individuals and support mortgage lenders in this process by buying the loans they originated.

Essentially, Fannie and Freddie operate behind the scenes, in the secondary mortgage market. They do not give direct mortgages to individuals. Instead, they use the process of mortgage securitization to fund mortgage lenders. Ultimately, their goal was to ensure liquidity in the mortgage industry.

Investors, who believe that Fannie and Freddie, like any other publicly traded company, are viable companies, are willing to buy their stocks and bonds. This is one way to raise capital. Fannie and Freddie then use this capital to purchase mortgages, which are then securitized and resold as investments.

As the housing decline continued with increased foreclosures, Fannie and Freddie suffered the consequences. On September 7, 2008, the Federal Housing Finance Agency (FHFA) placed both Fannie Mae and Freddie Mac in conservatorship. Under conservatorship, the FHFA took full control of the companies' assets. The U.S. Treasury put financing in place to ensure that Fannie and Freddie's financial obligations to bondholders would be honored and suspended all dividends to stockholders.[16]

Ginnie Mae (Government National Mortgage Association), unlike Fannie and Freddie, is government owned, and it has the full guarantee of the federal government. Additionally, it does not create and sell mortgage-backed securities. Rather, Ginnie Mae insures mortgage-backed securities created by government guaranteed agencies, such as the FHA (Federal Housing Administration). In the event of mortgage defaults, the lender can make a claim on the government agency's insurance; if the lender does not get full recovery from the insurance, Ginnie Mae makes up the difference. Ginnie Mae ensures that the investors in these MBSs will continue to receive their payments on a timely basis, regardless of the state of the underlying loan. Ginnie Mae- guaranteed MBSs are therefore considered safer investments than other MBSs.

SECURITIZATION

Typically, the only institutions affected by defaults on mortgages are the ones that gave the loans. As the financial system became more sophisticated, though, that changed. The use of mortgage-backed securities created a multiplier effect. Simply put, mortgages, both prime (good solid mortgages) and subprime (shaky and questionable) mortgages are packaged into securities. Investors purchase the securities, hoping for a return. Hence, the mortgages back the security, and it becomes a mortgage-backed security. Similarly, a share in a company backs the security we call a stock. These mortgages now have multiple owners—many investors own pieces of the bundled mortgages. It's like having twenty or more banks as the mortgage lender instead of one.

These securities are broken down into tranches, or issue groups, coded with letters, that represent different levels of riskiness. The subprime mortgages would have been in the tranche that carried the highest risk. Remember, the higher the risk, the greater the reward. The lettering indicates how credit rating agencies classify the securities. For example, the highest rating a bond can receive from a credit rating agency may be a triple A (AAA). The agencies rate everything from the safest bonds to so-called junk bonds. The rating level of a security will affect the magnitude of investment it attracts. An unrated bond is not likely to be purchased by the average investor, but a triple A (AAA) rated bond is considered a "safe" investment. Of course, it is only safe if the credit agency is actually correct.

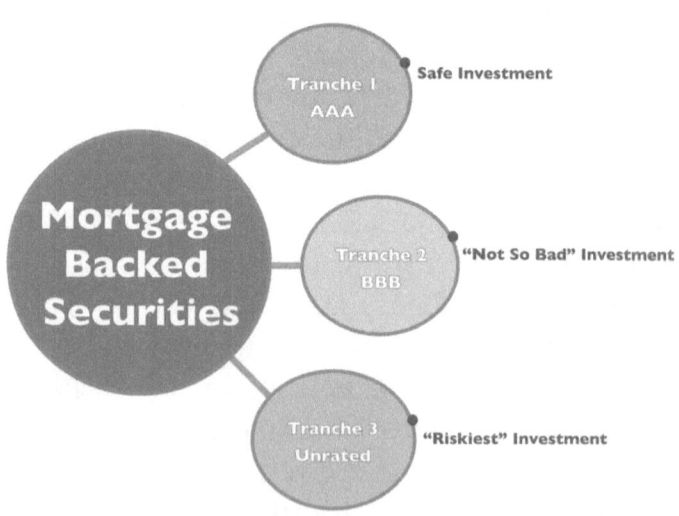

However, before we discuss the accuracy—or inaccuracy—of the rating agencies, we need to add one more layer to the stack of structured financial products, called collateralized debt obligations (CDOs).

CDOs are created by pooling assets, such as car loans, credit card debt, and other types of debt, into a securitized investment. Residential mortgage-backed CDOs, were created with residential MBSs as the underlying asset. These were split into tranches to be sold as bonds. It is basically the same process that was used to create MBSs from residential mortgages.

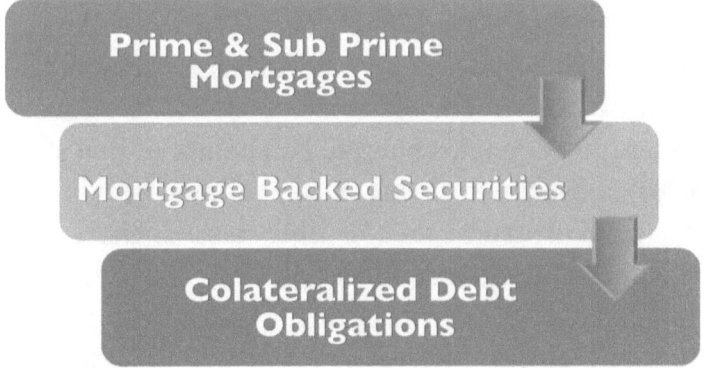

The resultant CDOs had to be rated by credit rating agencies, which again raises the question of accuracy. Rating agencies rate bonds based on the companies that issue the bonds. Therefore, using the same logic, the MBSs should be rated based on the types of borrowers who held the mortgages. However, there's a key difference: public corporations have to reveal their financial status quarterly and we can see their activities, but there was no way to see the financial status of the individuals who held the mortgages.

Therefore, the rating agencies had to use assumptions and financial models to come up with their ratings. Considering the credit downgrades of the CDOs and MBSs that occurred as mortgage defaults increased, the value of these products was actually anybody's guess.

Even more disturbing, however, is the fact that the rating agencies worked on behalf of the sellers of the securities, not the investors seeking guidance in making investment decisions. It used to be the case that rating agencies operated on behalf of investors who subscribed to them for ratings of various financial instruments. As time passed, there was a significant change in the process. It is now the financial services firms that pay the rating agencies to rate their products. It's easy to see the potential conflict of interest with this arrangement.

The investors took the risk that the mortgages that they invested in would be paid monthly, on time, and for the duration of the loan. As mortgage payments were received, they were passed on to the investors, less a fee, but if the homeowner defaulted on the loan or refinanced, the investor would lose.

So, why would anyone want to buy these CDOs and MBSs? If you invest in the stock of a company, you may do so thinking that the company is doing well financially, has a good image, is growing in market share, etc. You are taking a positive view of the company and gambling that, after you purchase the stock, its value, or price, will increase and therefore your value will increase. If you sell your stocks, you'll make a profit—referred to as capital gains, and you'll realize your investment goal. With mortgage-backed securities, the gamble an investor takes is that there will be no default on the mortgages—but, just in case, they often "hedge their position." Simply put, the investor insures the investment against the possibility of losses, which gives the investor some confidence in the position. Herein lies the topping on a scary sundae!

As the real estate market declined and the number of foreclosures increased, the mortgage industry was in trouble, along with the financial services industry. When mortgages started going bad, so did the value of the mortgage-backed securities. As they lost value and were downgraded by the financial rating agencies, it became apparent that, not only had the financial services industry come up with a fancy—and risky—product but it had also used a fancy "insurance policy" to protect against default: credit default swaps (CDS). I should point out, however, that the concept behind these products is not as risky as it seems in retrospect. The underlying security, subprime mortgages, is the true culprit. MBSs were successfully traded for years with prime mortgages as the underlying asset.

Credit default swaps became popular in the late 1990s, and their use grew rapidly. Essentially, a CDS is purchased by someone who owns an asset, for example, a mortgage-backed security, and who is concerned that the stream of payments may stop because of a default. As crazy as this may seem, a CDS may even be purchased by someone who doesn't own the asset for which default protection is being sought. This is done for speculation purposes, just to make money. The seller of the CDS promises to pay that person whatever value the policy says should be paid. This might seem similar to any insurance policy, but it's not. The difference is, the CDSs are not issued as traditional insurance policies, and they are not subject to government regulations. Unlike insurance companies that are required to keep reserves of a certain percentage of their exposure (benefits to be paid from policies), the entities that created and sold CDSs had no such requirements to meet.

When a CDS was sold, the seller *was* required to put up collateral, but it was not at the same threshold as a regulated insurance company. The seller of the policy also received a fee or premium payment. This was a great source of income for the institutions that sold CDSs. In the event that there was no payout, they got around 2 percent of the insured value, free and clear. It was also expected that, since sellers of CDSs were assuming risk, they ought to protect themselves by entering into a swap to hedge their risk in the event of a payout. So who were some of the major players? To name a few—AIG, Lehman Brothers, and Bear Stearns. It's no coincidence that they are all at the center of the 2008 financial collapse.

There is actually another component to this mix: leverage. During the financial meltdown, we heard the term leverage over and over. In its simplest form, leverage is using other people's money. We use leverage in our everyday lives when we use credit cards, for example. Borrowing is a very popular, and highly recommended, way to do business. Why use your own money when you can borrow someone else's? Borrow at an interest rate that is lower than the one you receive from whatever you've invested in— and the difference is your profit. This is a culture in business and is nothing unusual. However, within the derivative markets, leveraging goes beyond the mere borrowing of money, it involves the use of trading strategies that are often times risky, but if the gamble pays off, it will be beneficial to the investing firm.

Unfortunately, many large financial firms were highly leveraged in the securitized mortgage market, and then, to make matters worse, the underlying "property"—the mortgages behind the securities—lost its value. The house of cards started to fall. So, how were they able to do this?

1.　Money was cheap! The monetary policy of the Fed was to keep interest rates low in an effort to keep the credit market liquid. This allowed individuals and corporations alike to get loans at low interest rates.

2.　To further complicate matters, the credit rating agencies were not able to appropriately "grade" the investments, so the true risk of these products were not reflected in their ratings.

3.　Most of the financial products that the investment banks bought and sold were considered "off balance sheet" items. This means that they were not represented clearly in the published financial reports of the firms.

As the value of these MBSs dwindled, heavily leveraged financial services firms did not have the money to satisfy their positions in the derivative markets. Likewise, the sellers of the CDSs didn't have the money to pay the claims on these policies. The widespread nature of these speculative investments fueled a dangerous fire that spread to touch the lives of many people in the United States and globally.

TROUBLED ASSET RELIEF PROGRAM (TARP)

The first major institution to fail was Bear Sterns. This failure started the nationwide discussion of whether to bail out failing institutions. When the government decided to bail out some large financial institutions, there was rhyme and reason behind this decision. In retrospect, it can be said that some of the decisions made possibly should have gone in the other direction, but there are no perfect solutions in this imperfect world.

However, in solving problems, the best approach is to peel away at the layers of an issue until the core problem is found. Once that is done, thought should be given to identifying what caused the problem and how it can be fixed. Anything less would be like applying a bandage to an open wound and pretending it is just a scratch. If the problem is wrongly diagnosed, the solution implemented will certainly fail because it is not addressing the *real* problem.

So, we had a problem: the economy was on the verge of collapse. With little time to spare, the government splashed the "wound" with a little antiseptic. Lehman Brothers was allowed to fail, because that is what capitalism should allow. It stung a little bit—but might have made things worse. Next, a bandage was applied to keep the wound covered and start the healing process: the Emergency Economic Stabilization Act of 2008, infused with the antibiotic TARP. Was that sufficient?

TARP, the Troubled Asset Relief Program, was implemented primarily to purchase or insure the "toxic assets" that were in the possession of many financial institutions. The term *toxic assets* refers to financial products that were backed by residential mortgages that no longer held much value as the crisis deepened. Armed with $700 billion to execute its mission of stabilization, the Treasury Department created several programs within TARP to address different areas of concern. According to the Government Accountability Office,[17] the largest program is the Capital Purchase Program (CPP), which, as of September 11, 2009, had provided more than $200 billion in capital to financial institutions. The CPP represents approximately 56 percent of the total TARP disbursements to this point. Other major programs in place are as follows:

- TALF (Term Asset-Backed Securities Loan Facility)—The purpose of this program is to restart the securitization markets. We now know that activity within these markets contributed to the instability and near collapse of our financial system. However, the process of securitization does create opportunities for financial institutions to offer loans. Credit still remains essential to the growth of our economy, but, it is hoped that credit will be offered within more carefully defined parameters.

- HAMP (Home Affordable Modification Program)—This program is designed to support the modification of residential mortgages in an effort to stem the foreclosure crisis, stabilize the housing market, and, of course reduce the number of displaced families and the accompanying social effects. One of the main problems this program faces is ensuring that the loan modification decisions process, whether the modification is approved or denied, is transparent to the borrowers. Another issue is establishing internal controls to oversee the participating firms' compliance with the program guidelines.

- SSFI (Systemically Significant Failing Institutions program)—This program has been designed to assist financial institutions that are considered systemically significant and whose failure could be disruptive to the industry and the wider economy. As of September 11, 2009, American International Group (AIG) was the only institution participating in this program. As of that date, $43.2 billion has been disbursed, of $70 billion in TARP funding that was committed to AIG. Participation in this program will be determined by the Treasury Department on a case–by-case basis.

The biggest uncertainty surrounding TARP is deciding whether it has been successful. Arguments supporting both views have been made: On one hand, there has not been another failure of a major financial institution since the government intervened. On the other hand, the argument can be made that the credit markets have not improved significantly enough to call the intervention a success. From all indications, this will be a slow recovery process.

MAJOR PLAYERS

THEIR ROLES AND THE RESULTS

Throughout this book, I have looked at critical regulatory changes and how they were influenced by financial institutions and the government. This section will look at some specific institutions, describe their roles in the financial crisis, and look at what the consequences have been for these firms.

The very public discussion of the bailout focuses on the $700 billion in TARP funding that was hastily approved by Congress. However, there are additional "backstop" measures to protect institutions from additional losses from toxic assets. For example, though Bank of America already received $45 billion in TARP funds, the company also has a $118 billion backstop facility, which means that the government will provide assistance with future Merrill Lynch losses if they exceed $10 billion.[18]

As of November 6, 2009, one hundred and twenty commercial banks had failed. Most of them were not known nationally, but there were a few well-known banks that were absorbed by larger banks. On September 26, 2008, the FDIC sold Washington Mutual Bank to JPMorgan Chase. This move triggered a run on Wachovia. Wachovia, significantly weakened, was sold to Wells Fargo on October 12, 2009, after a battle with Citigroup. Both Washington Mutual and Wachovia were heavily invested in the mortgage market and the securitized products.

Goldman Sachs was thought to be the ultimate example of a successful securities and investment firm on Wall Street—until the financial crisis. It then converted itself into a bank holding company. This sudden conversion, in September 2008, was made so that the company could take advantage of the TARP bailout. However, even without its conversion, Goldman was an indirect beneficiary of the bailout through AIG. AIG was required to pay counterparties for CDSs. Goldman Sachs was one of AIG's counterparties, and it was paid after AIG received its bailout. Goldman Sachs also suffered from investor withdrawals and the resulting downward pressure on its stock price. Ultimately, the firm opted to position itself to receive temporary government aid. Goldman received $10 billion from TARP.

BEAR STEARNS

March 2008 was not a good month for Bear Stearns, then an eighty-five-year-old investment bank. The firm posted a major loss at the end of 2007, forcing the resignation of the CEO. Bear Stearns was in trouble. The company's troubles started when two hedge funds they owned failed in 2007. These funds were heavily invested in subprime mortgage products and Bear Stearns had injected funding to keep them afloat. It didn't work. Using its own mortgage holdings, Bear Stearns entered into a hedging strategy to protect itself as the housing market took a downward turn and subprime mortgage-backed securities were downgraded by credit rating agencies.

Bear Stearns attempted and failed to secure equity injections from major investors. The combination of the mortgage crisis and the lack of new equity injections added pressure to Bear Stearns's ability to remain viable. Essentially, banks were hesitant to continue lending to Bear Stearns because a significant portion of the company's assets was high risk. Uncertainty about Bear Stearns's future fueled a pullback from lenders. This led to a liquidity crisis for the investment giant. Bear Stearns did not have the cash to operate from day to day. To further compound the problem, investors started pulling their money from the company. In a matter of days, this giant was brought to its knees.

In a weekend mad dash, a hurried buyout was organized by JPMorgan Chase, with an assist by the Federal Reserve. The goal was to save Bear Stearns, somehow, to avoid major repercussions in the financial markets.

The Federal Reserve loaned JPMorgan Chase close to $30 billion to purchase Bear Stearns at a mere ten dollars per share. This was unfortunate for the Bear Stearns stockholders—only a year earlier, the price of Bear Stearns stock was $152.97 per share. Prior to the final agreement, JPMorgan had offered $2 per share, at a time when the shares were trading at approximately $30, having already suffered significant declines due to industry speculation about an impending failure. It now appears that this lowball offer put further downward pressure on the stock price, and its value plunged to a mere $4.81.[19] Significant value for Bear Stearns clients as well as shareholders was lost during this tumultuous time and, ultimately, in this transaction.

Saving Bear Stearns was a valiant attempt to calm the financial markets. The last thing our financial system needed was a widespread state of panic. However, this was not to be; panic came anyway, and Lehman Brothers was the next target.

LEHMAN BROTHERS

The fall of Lehman Brothers took approximately one year, culminating in the firm's bankruptcy on September 15, 2008. This unfortunate end was a result of over-investment in mortgage-backed securities. Once the mortgage industry started faltering, major losses were inevitable for Lehman Brothers. As reported by *The New York Times* on June 9, 2008, Lehman posted a second-quarter loss of $2.8 billion.[20] This loss fueled concerns about the long-term viability of the firm—after that, negotiations to raise capital were futile.

In true Wall Street style, if a company seems likely to fail, some investors turn to strategies that will pay them when the company fails. This is called selling the stock short. In essence, an investor would borrow the stock from a broker and sell it in the market with the expectation that the price will go down. In a successful short, the investor can repurchase the stocks at a lower price and return them to the broker. The profit is in the spread between the two transactions. This is an investment strategy that has been used quite successfully, and it is based on the economic principle of supply and demand. All other things being constant, with excess supply, the price of a product will go down.

In addition to short selling, there is the issue of creating doubt to ensure that the stock price will decline. With the fall of Bear Stearns and the potential fall of Lehman Brothers, rumors ran wild on Wall Street about the internal problems these firms were having with cash flow. This drove investors to close accounts and sell off shares they held, which added fuel to the fire and made the companies' problems worse.

Unfortunately for Lehman Brothers, the Federal Reserve did not step in to help the firm avert bankruptcy, as it had for Bear Stearns. Lehman Brothers got no bailout. Henry Paulson, then Treasury Secretary, argued that the company did not have sufficient assets to collateralize an intervention (AIG would fare better). In the end, Lehman Brothers filed for bankruptcy, and its divisions were sold separately to other institutions, including Barclays, a British bank. However, while Lehman Brothers did not get a bailout, they did receive a short-term loan from the Fed through JPMorgan Chase. This loan was specifically issued to help close current trades in a way that would not completely disrupt the operations of other financial institutions.

Why was Lehman Brothers allowed to fail? This failure did throw the financial markets into a tailspin—the very event the government was trying to avoid. One year later, the answer is still not clear, though the healing process has begun. Until the real issues are dealt with, we'll never truly stand on a firm footing to move forward.

AMERICAN INTERNATIONAL GROUP (AIG)

On September 16, 2008, one day after the Lehman Brothers bankruptcy, the federal government loaned AIG $85 billion to stem its liquidity crisis. AIG's problems were also related to mortgage-backed securities and credit default swaps.

AIG, the world's largest insurance company, is less known for its financial products division, AIGFP. This division sold over $400 billion of credit default swaps to institutions that needed default protection.[21] AIG also held mortgage-backed securities in its own corporate portfolio. With the downturn in the real estate market and the increase in foreclosure rates, mortgage-backed securities started to lose value. These securities had to be marked down to reflect their true market value; this resulted in major losses for any company holding them, including

AIG. These losses, along with credit risk exposure from the CDS business, triggered a downgrade in AIG's credit rating.

When a company purchases a CDS contract to protect itself from the risk of default, it does so on the premise that the seller, the insurer, is financially healthy. To ensure that purchasers are getting real protection, the contracts usually call for collateral to be posted in the event of a downgrade in the credit rating of the company. A downgrade in a company's credit rating is an indication of the deterioration in the soundness of its financial position. Thus, when AIG's credit rating was downgraded, a collateral call was made. AIG found itself in dire straits.

Several crucial events: a write down in asset values, payout on CDS contracts, and collateral calls, occurring together created the dangerous cocktail of a liquidity crunch. If this major player in the financial sector was suffering a liquidity crisis, in the aftermath of the failures of Bear Stearns and Lehman Brothers, what lender, considering their fiduciary duty to their investors, would lend AIG money to fix the problem? None. This was not only a problem for AIG, but it was a problem for many other companies in various sectors of the economy—a freeze had begun in the credit markets, which meant that lenders were severely curtailing their lending.

In response to AIG's liquidity problem, the federal government intervened by injecting cash into AIG to prevent a complete collapse. It has been argued that this federal loan was absolutely necessary because of the size of AIG—too big to fail. Since the initial bailout, there has been some restructuring of the federal loan, changing the type of shares "we"— the taxpayers who underwrote the loan—own. The shares have been changed from cumulative preferred shares to preferred shares "that more closely resemble common equity."[22] AIG will also be able to raise up to an additional $30 billion by selling noncumulative preferred stock to the U.S. Treasury. What does all of that mean?

It means that the deal the government made with AIG has changed to take the pressure off of AIG. Common stock is what most of us buy when we participate in the stock market. It is the most basic form of ownership in a company, also referred to as equity in the company. A common stock owner may receive dividend payments if the company has made a profit, has made all interest payments to bond holders, and has paid dividends to preferred stock holders. Owners of common stock are the last to get paid in the event that the company goes bankrupt and dissolves. The bright side is that the common stockholder has voting rights. On the other hand, preferred stockholders can either be participating or non-participating, and cumulative or noncumulative, preferred stockholders.

The difference between participating and non-participating is in promised versus actual dividends. A participating preferred stock may pay out a higher dividend than promised, based on reported profits. On the other hand, a non-participating preferred stock will pay a fixed dividend, as agreed when it was issued. A cumulative preferred stock simply means that, if the company is unable to pay dividends at the time it should, those dividends are accumulated and paid out at a later date. To own noncumulative preferred shares is the opposite—if a dividend distribution is not possible, shareholders simply wait until the next dividend is due, with no compensation for the missed payment. In return, non-cumulative preferred stock owners get voting rights. In most instances, however, preferred stocks are cumulative and non-participating.

Let's review: the AIG shares that the U.S. taxpayers own are now more like common shares rather than preferred shares. AIG may sell up to $30 billion in noncumulative preferred shares to the U.S. Treasury. In essence, we have assumed more risk, and the pressure is off AIG to make dividend payments to their most important investor—the American taxpayer. Wow!

These actions, along with the sale of individual business units, are part of the strategy to stabilize AIG and help the insurance giant turn a profit, so that it can repay the taxpayers. I think the government's intervention was necessary, but the devil is in the details, and it is a tough pill to swallow.

CITIGROUP

In our earlier discussion, the merger of Citicorp and Travelers Group was cited as a major trigger for financial modernization legislation and was the advent of organizations deemed "too big to fail."

Citigroup, commonly referred to as Citi, was heavily involved in the securitized mortgage market and suffered tremendously as the bottom fell out of the market. Citi posted losses of $7.6 billion in its Securities and Banking segment for 2007,[23] as it incurred write downs from the diminishing value of subprime mortgage products and other derivatives, now called "toxic assets." Overall, the company was still profitable in 2007. However, in response to obvious financial difficulties, old management wisdom dictates that a company must cut costs and increase revenue to improve profitability. Unfortunately, cutting costs usually leads to a reduction in human resources: Citigroup cut approximately 52,000 jobs in 2008. Citi also reduced other operating expenses and raised capital from private investors and the government. However, despite these actions, Citi suffered a remarkable overall consolidated loss of $27.7 billion for 2008.[24]

With the financial system in jeopardy of collapse from major losses and a frozen credit market, the government injected $49 billion of TARP funds into Citigroup. According to the U.S. Treasury's November 6, 2009 report on TARP,[25] Citi received funds from three programs: the Capital Purchase Program, the Asset Guarantee Program, and the Targeted Investment Program.

Citigroup has since divested many of its businesses, and it has even sold its retail brokerage business, Smith Barney. It did turn a profit of $101 million in the third quarter of 2009, compared with 2008's third-quarter results of a $2.8 billion loss[26], and on December 14, 2009, Citi announced that it will be repaying the government $20 billion in TARP funds.

It will be interesting to see where Citigroup is as this crisis fades into the background and the economy stabilizes. Citigroup, under previous management, pushed to create complex "one-stop-shop" financial firms. A decade later, we are witnessing the slow unwinding of this conglomerate, an event that sends a clear message that this strategy may not be the best strategy for long-term growth and prosperity.

MERRILL LYNCH &
BANK OF AMERICA

Merrill Lynch, formed in 1914, is one of the oldest and largest brokerage houses worldwide. The company was divided into two major divisions: global wealth management and investment banking. The unfortunate fate awaiting this giant was the unraveling of the financial web of securitization. Like other firms at the center of the financial crisis, Merrill Lynch was heavily invested in structured mortgage-backed products, and the company suffered tremendous losses as the crisis progressed and it sold off some of its assets at less than the value they were carried at on the books.

In 2008, Merrill reported a net loss of $27.6 billion, almost $20 billion more than the previous year.[27] By the end of 2008, it was evident that this financial giant was heading toward the same fate as Bear Sterns and Lehman Brothers if immediate action wasn't taken. A now familiar, hastily assembled merger and acquisition deal took place, and Merrill Lynch, an independent, well established powerhouse, ceased to exist.

On September 15, 2008, Bank of America announced that it had agreed to purchase Merrill Lynch.[28] On December 5, 2008, that acquisition was approved by the Merrill Lynch stockholders, who agreed to take 85.95 percent of the number of common stocks they held in Merrill Lynch in Bank of America common stocks. So if they had 100 Merrill shares, after the acquisition, they would hold 85.95 Bank of America shares. The good news for Merrill investors was that Bank of America stocks closed at $15.24 on December 5, 2008 and Merrill Lynch closed at $13.04, meaning that the exchange was just about even.

The unfortunate circumstances surrounding this acquisition actually go beyond the impact on Merrill Lynch and its stockholders, though, and concern the impact on Bank of America and its stockholders. Based on testimony to Congress, Bank of America had decided that the acquisition was no longer in the company's best interest, but it found itself pressured by the Fed to go through with the deal. This acquisition "creates a company unrivalled in its breadth of financial services and global reach" according to a Merrill Lynch press release on September 15, 2008. The merger created another super financial institution that will undoubtedly be considered too big to fail. We saw this with the mega-merger that created Citigroup, and we have since seen its slow unwinding. Will this be the future for Bank of America?

As the debate continues about the level of the government's involvement in the deal, Bank of America has found itself under federal investigation for withholding information from its stockholders pertaining to the losses that Merrill Lynch brought to the table. Again, in formal testimony to Congress, it has been suggested that the Bank of America CEO was encouraged by the chairmen of the Federal Reserve and the U.S. Treasury to withhold the full extent of Merrill's financial troubles because, if the acquisition deal was not completed, the financial crisis could become even more severe. I will refrain from commenting on the situation beyond stating these basic allegations, because this is a legal issue that has not yet been resolved.

Bank of America has so far received $45 billion in TARP funds; it has assumed two troubled businesses in one year—mortgage giant Countrywide and brokerage giant Merrill Lynch. It is now possibly the largest financial institution in the world, and it is under ethical and legal scrutiny. In the short term, acquisition of Merrill Lynch *may* have prevented additional instability in the financial system, but at the point when it becomes too hard to manage, too hard to regulate, and too big to fail, will it, in turn, destabilize the economy?

HEDGE FUNDS

A hedge fund is generally an aggressive investment fund that produces higher returns than other funds because it usually engages in riskier investments. Hedge funds are privately operated and largely unregulated. Therefore, fund managers or owners are not required to publicly disclose the results of their operations. Additionally, by keeping the number of investors below one hundred, hedge funds avoid being regulated. While they are not required to register with the Securities and Exchange Commission (SEC), they are still subject to laws governing fraud.

In order to qualify as a client, you must meet the definition an accredited investor, who is an individual with minimum assets of $1 million.[29] Investors who do not meet these criteria, or who choose not to invest directly into a hedge fund, may invest in funds of hedge funds, an option available at much lower levels of initial investment. According to the SEC, "a fund of a hedge fund is an investment company that invests in hedge funds rather than investing in individual securities."[30] Some of these investment companies do register with the SEC and are regulated accordingly.

One of the components of the2008 financial crisis was the level of leveraging that was used to generate super returns. Leveraging is the use of borrowed money. The aim is to borrow at a low interest rate, invest the funds, and, one hopes, generate a much higher return in order to repay the borrowed funds and make a profit. Leverage is a standard practice in business, but excessive leverage creates a cause for concern. Hedge funds use leverage to fund highly speculative strategies—foreign exchange (for-ex) trading, options, swaps, futures, etc.—which will either generate great profits or painfully significant losses. Hedge funds that fall within certain parameters are not registered with the SEC, and therefore they are not required to disclose their transactions. For these reasons, their sources of funding and how much leverage they are actually using are not generally known.

In 1998, Long Term Capital Management (LTCM), a hedge fund, created waves in the financial services industry when it teetered on the brink of failure. LTCM's failure would have had a domino effect, triggering many other institutional failures. Leverage played a significant role in the fund's demise, as it was determined that LTCM had a leverage ratio of 25:1, based on its January 1, 1998 balance sheet.[31] This means that LTCM had 25 times more in debt than it had in assets it owned. The use of such high leverage, combined with the changes in Russia's financial landscape—in which the fund was heavily invested—triggered the near collapse of the hedge fund.

The response from the government then was very much like it was in 2008: we cannot allow this firm to fail. While the government did not directly provide a bailout to LTCM, it orchestrated the process of bolstering the failing hedge fund. Again, investors in the fund lost significant value in the transaction, but the firm did not fail, and the Fed managed to stem systemic failure with its intervention.

What was the state of hedge funds in 2008–2009? *The New York Times* reported on October 23, 2008[32] that hedge funds had lost $180 billion in the previous three months. In addition, we have seen the uncovering of a far-reaching Ponzi scheme created by Bernie Madoff, a former chairman of the NASDAQ, despite the fact that he was registered with the SEC. Most recently, in October 2009, we saw the arrest of the co-founder of Galleon Group Hedge Fund for insider trading. Hedge funds will rebound; however, I believe that they ought to be regulated and required to operate within enforced boundaries.

GETTING BEYOND THE CRISIS

THE PROPOSAL

"The more things change, the more they remain the same."

Is that what we have to look forward to? Or will we see real and effective solutions at this pivotal time? The current administration has proposed the financial reforms that it thinks will be necessary to restore the integrity and stability of our financial services industry.

The United States Department of Treasury, in its document *Financial Regulatory Reform: A New Foundation*,[33] offers several recommendations, most of which will be deliberated and debated in Congress. This chapter presents each of these recommendations, along with greater detail about how these would be accomplished, including increased layers of bureaucracy and government control. Most of the proposed systems would be managed or supervised by the Treasury Department, the Federal Reserve, or both. Some suggestions have already sparked opposition within the financial industry and within the halls of public debate. I strongly recommend that everyone reading this book should read the entire proposal and follow closely as the debate unfolds.

Broadly, the recommendations are as follows:

1. **Promote robust supervision and regulation of financial firms.**

   The recommendation is to establish a Financial Services Oversight Council to coordinate information and identify firms that pose systemic risks to the financial industry because of their size, level of leverage, and interconnectedness. It is proposed that the Council be chaired by the Secretary of the Treasury and that it include the Chairman of the Board of Governors of the Federal Reserve System and the heads of other high-level regulatory bodies. These large interconnected firms are known as Tier 1 Financial Holding Companies (FHCs). In addition to the Council's role in coordinating and sharing information on the Tier 1 FHCs, there is a call for consolidated and stricter supervision of these firms and for increased capital requirements. It is separately noted in these recommendations that the guidelines on capital requirements should not be limited to subsidiary depository institutions but should apply to the FHC as a consolidated entity.

Given the widespread global trauma caused by the financial crisis, it is crucial to close loopholes that exist in our legislation. The proposal specifically says, "The policy separating banking from commerce should be reaffirmed and strengthened. We must close loopholes in the BHC Act for thrift holding companies, industrial loan companies, credit card banks, trust companies, and grandfathered "nonbank" banks." In this area, the Treasury recommends that a new federal agency, called the National Bank Supervisor, be created to supervise and regulate "all federally chartered depository institutions and all federal branches and agencies of foreign banks." While a new federal agency has been proposed, the elimination of one is on the table for consideration: the federal thrift charter, facilitated through the Office of Thrift Supervision (OTS), is faced with elimination under these proposals.

The shadow banking system, institutions that operate off the radar of regulatory agencies, has created cause for concern— and with good reason. In addressing this problem, the Treasury recommends that hedge funds and other private pools of capital register with the SEC. The advisors to these funds would be required to report on the funds they manage for risk assessment purposes.

2. **Establish comprehensive regulation of financial markets.**

The most poignant issue to address here is the regulation of the securitization markets. We already looked at the crucial role these markets played in the financial crisis. It is imperative that action be quickly taken in this area. The recommendation is to require the issuers of securitized products to maintain an interest in the product as well. Therefore, the risk is not completely borne by the investor. Securitization markets have been criticized as lacking transparency; the recommendations put the burden on the SEC to increase the transparency and standardization of these markets, along with the rating agencies, whose stamp of credibility may have been misleading.

The other major area of concern is the over-the-counter derivative markets. Credit default swaps were responsible for the near collapse of AIG's financial division. These products have been trading in a fairly unregulated marketplace, which has now come under scrutiny. The proposal calls for comprehensive regulation that would, among other things, "prevent activities in those markets from posing risk to the financial system." Regulation and transparency in these markets would accomplish this.

3. **Protect consumers and investors from financial abuse.**

The creation of a new Consumer Financial Protection Agency (CFPA) is the overarching recommendation in this area. This new agency would protect consumers of financial products and regulate the providers of these products and services. It is proposed that this new agency be independent and have sole authority to make rules for consumer financial protection statutes. The CFPA would be expected to create transparency, simplicity, fairness, and access to financial information, products, and services.

4. Provide the government with the tools it needs to manage financial crises.

In light of the crisis management saga we witnessed in September 2008, this recommendation seems appropriate. The Treasury is proposing that a resolution regime be created to handle the orderly dissolution of financial institutions, especially the Tier 1 FHCs that could pose serious risk to the entire financial system. This would be in addition to the FDIC, which is already in place to handle the resolution of failing depository institutions. The proposal also calls for a legislative amendment that would allow the Fed, with written approval from the Treasury Secretary, to extend credit to entities in "unusual and exigent circumstances." I interpret this to mean that, if the Federal Reserve and the Secretary of the Treasury feel that an entity is too big to fail, they can extend credit to that entity.

5. Raise international regulatory standards and improve international cooperation.

The tragic reality of the economic crisis is that it was not limited to the United States. Global financial interconnectedness goes beyond the firms we easily identify on Wall Street and in other metropolitan centers. Globalization has its pros and cons. The domino effect of the bank failures in the United States that stretched across the world is one of the cons. The recommendations made by the United States Treasury on these issues become more complicated in the international arena because, though we have strong influence, we are not the only decision makers.

Some of the major recommendations include strengthening the international capital framework through the Basel II capital requirements; improving oversight and standardization of the over-the-counter derivative markets; enhancing supervision of internationally active financial firms; expediting the efforts of the Basel Committee on Banking Supervision (BCBS) to improve cross-border resolution of global financial firms; expanding the scope of regulation by appropriately defining Tier 1 FHC status and applying the requirements to foreign financial firms; and urging other countries to implement the G-20 commitment to requiring hedge funds, or their managers, to register and disclose information that is needed to assess risk.

This discussion was a synopsis of the Treasury's recommendations. I urge you to visit the Treasury Department's website, www.financialstability.gov, for the detailed proposal.

THE CONCERNS

Many concerns about these proposals have been voiced by individuals, academics, and organized bodies that represent specific groups. Here, I present my concerns along with some concerns raised by the American Bankers Association. First, here are my concerns:

- In addressing regulatory shortcomings, new loopholes may be created in the attempt to close the existing ones. Seems like that's the way these things often work. Will it be different this time? I am not holding my breath while we wait to see how Congress handles this issue.

- We already had what should have been sufficient regulation in place with the Financial Modernization Act, but the rules were evidently not well enforced. We had different regulators for FHCs based on the functional areas. This meant that individual functional areas were regulated separately, but the complete collage of information never came together. The recommendations outlined by Treasury suggest a more consolidated approach to regulation, but there are still a number of agencies involved. It makes me a little nervous to think that this may be a case of "the more things change, the more they remain the same."

- A new consumer protection agency adds one more layer of bureaucracy, but will it be beneficial to consumers? It can be, if everything works according to the plan on paper. The problem is, things don't always go according to plan. This new agency could add an unnecessary and inefficient layer to the systems and processes already in place.

- We have in place the FDIC to resolve failing depository institutions but the magnitude of failures in 2008 was beyond the capacity of that agency to address. The government now proposes to put in place systems that will allow quick and decisive response to any institutional failure that could pose a serious threat to the economy. This is the indicator, in my opinion, that the concept of "too big to fail" may be here to stay. Unless these mega-companies are required to break apart into separate, distinct divisions, we could be faced with additional potentially catastrophic failures that we would be forced to prevent.

- In April 2009, the G20 Summit was held in London, England to discuss the global financial crisis. Participants in the summit made commitments to work toward a mutually beneficial global regulatory framework that could meet the needs of the global community. I anticipate that some of the U.S proposals will be adopted internationally, but it's hard enough to get Congress to agree on the best approach; it will be that much harder to get agreement from nations separated by land, sea, culture, and more.

Members of the banking industry have voiced their opposition to some of these proposals as well:

- The American Bankers Association (ABA) makes a compelling argument that increased regulation of traditional banks could prove to be burdensome to institutions that did not create the conditions leading to the systemic failures. In his testimony to the House Financial Services Committee on July 15, the ABA president stated, "Thousands of banks of all sizes, in communities across the country, are scared to death that their already crushing regulatory burdens will be increased dramatically by regulations aimed primarily at their less-regulated or unregulated competitors."[34] The question is: will the good suffer for the bad? Again, Congress will debate these issues and we should follow closely to see how these valid objections are addressed. While I think that it is unfortunate that small, community-based banks could be saddled with new regulations, I am concerned that the negotiations and compromises will create loopholes that will be found and exploited by other financial institutions.

- The ABA strongly opposes the proposed elimination of the OTS, which was established in 1989 to supervise, charter, and regulate the thrift industry.[35] The

ABA's objection is based on the premise that thrift institutions were not, for the most part, participants in the subprime mortgage lending practice that led to the mortgage crisis. Additionally, the ABA is concerned that establishing a new charter will:[36]

- generate unnecessary costs to the thrift institutions in the form of increased operational expenses that are created with a charter change;

- deny potential homeowners the expertise of professionals trained under a thrift charter;

- ignore the historical importance of the thrift charter in championing the cause of home ownership; and

- *not* solve the problems that caused the crisis.

This is a brief summary of the concerns voiced by the American Bankers Association; I encourage every reader to delve into the details, which can be found at www.aba.com.

THE FINAL WORD

CONCLUSION

The question remains: was the financial bailout of Wall Street a necessary evil or just plain evil?

While I suggest that you decide for yourself, I would argue that perhaps it was both. Let me explain.

I believe that without the intervention of the United States government, the financial crisis would have spiraled into a catastrophe that none of us would want to suffer through. As the financial crisis developed and deepened, it did cause suffering for a tremendous number of people and institutions around the world. So, while it seems evil to force taxpayers to carry the burden of the bailout, the bailout was necessary to prevent even more suffering. However, what I regard as just plain evil is the fact that private institutions were allowed to become so large and crucial to the economy that they were "too big to fail."

"The love of money is the root of all evil" is a Biblical reference we've often heard quoted, and sometimes misquoted as, *"money is the root of all evil."* I dare say that Wall Street outdid itself, undermining the credibility of the American economy and government in the process. I've concluded from my research that the perpetual drive of Wall Street firms to make more money and pay ever-higher salaries and bonuses drove the excessively risky mortgage lending practices. Greed was behind the push to securitize more mortgages and then to securitize those securitized mortgages. However, Wall Street firms are not alone in their culpability for the crisis.

The legislative arm of our government, Congress, is also at fault for not putting in place legislation to prevent this perfect storm from developing. In fact, Congress has progressively enacted legislation that gave Wall Street more opportunity and autonomy to aggressively pursue profits.

I support the free market economy and the ability of businesses to succeed and profit. However, it is important to recognize that, while financial institutions play a leading role in the free market, they do so in pursuit of their own interests and profits! I believe that the profit objective can be achieved within parameters that are healthy for the businesses and the stakeholders.

Not only did our legislative arm empower Wall Street, it empowered two government-sponsored entities, Fannie Mae and Freddie Mac, to extend and expand home ownership in the United States. While the concept is good, the process failed the people. There is no excuse for the subprime lending practices that inevitably led to staggering numbers of home foreclosures. While Fannie and Freddie were not the only perpetrators of that practice, I do not doubt that their participation was driven by the profit motive.

The Federal Reserve should not go without blame either. The Federal Reserve kept the fed funds target rate low, which meant that money was cheap. As in the retail business, demand is fueled by low prices—interest rates, in the case of money supply. Easy access to credit inflamed the insatiable desire of financiers to use leverage as a money-making tool. While we're pointing fingers of blame at Wall Street firms, we must remember that the government enabled them.

An additional major stakeholder in this perfect storm is us—consumers and taxpayers. Whether directly through personal investment accounts or indirectly through retirement accounts that are invested on our behalf, collectively we demand the success and profitability of Wall Street. We all want a piece of the pie. We are all affected by the success or failure of the economy. We all have a vested interest: the companies we work for, the local banks we do business with, the universities we want our children to attend—all are part of the financial investment picture.

In a quest to secure their piece of the American dream, many Americans were sucked into the mesmerizing whirlpool of subprime mortgages. Some were fooled, others were foolish. Not only did individuals assume mortgages they could not afford and did not understand, but many more took on credit card debt that gave new definition to "living beyond your means." Not only are families struggling to stay in their homes, many are defaulting on their credit card obligations. So yes, "we the people" were active participants in the demise of the economy. That means that we, as stakeholders, have the personal responsibility to pay attention to what is happening on Wall Street and Congress from here onward. We have a responsibility to ourselves to keep informed and to hold our elected officials accountable.

The dilemma we now face is that, as financial institutions struggle to stay afloat, some are gobbled up by larger institutions, and the assets of those that have failed are bought, at great deals, by other large financial institutions. The resulting consolidation within the financial services industry is creating even larger institutions that will continue to be critical to the economy. Yet we have not enacted any *real* solutions. I believe it is fair to say that it is irresponsible to allow such enormous organizations to exist, especially after the significant investment that "we the people" had to make in those businesses to avert further failures.

The significant financial intervention by the government should never have to happen again. Unfortunately, the Troubled Assets Relief Program, while necessary in concept, has set a precedent. While it was not the first time that the government has come to the rescue of financial institutions, it was certainly a first in its magnitude. Unless there are sustainable changes to the regulatory framework to oversee aspects of the financial services industry that operated unchecked and efforts to better enforce existing regulations, we will be talking about another financial crisis in the future.

As I have suggested, there can be success and profitability without the level of systemic risk we saw in this crisis. *A warning*: such a system is not likely to come with the bounty that prevailed in the years prior to the meltdown. There is a cost for the genius of financial engineering that produced those high returns, and we are living with that cost now. I say simply: any institution that is too big to fail is too big to exist. Something has got to give.

This is actually *not* my final word. Let's keep the conversation going. Visit: <u>www.whytoobigtofail.com</u>.

NOTES

1. C. D. Romer, *Great Depression,* http://elsa.berkeley.edu/~cromer/great_depression.pdf.
2. Federal Deposit Insurance Corporation, *Temporary Changes to FDIC Deposit Insurance Coverage,* August 27, 2009, http://www.fdic.gov/deposit/Deposits/insured/index.html.
3. Jonathan Zubrow Cohen, "The Mellon Bank Order: An Unjustifiable Expansion of Banking Powers," *Washington College of Law, The American University Administrative Law Journal,* Summer 1994.
4. Federal Deposit Insurance Corporation, *History of the Eighties-Lessons for the Future, Vol. 1: An Examination of the Banking Crises of the 1980s and Early 1990s,* Chapter 4, December 1997.
5. ibid.
6. ibid., Chapter 2.
7. ibid., Chapter 4.
8. Jerry W. Markham, "Banking Regulation: Its History and Future," *University of North Carolina School of Law Banking Institute, North Carolina Banking Institute,* April 2000.
9. ibid.
10. Federal Reserve System, *Revenue Limit on Bank –Ineligible Activities of Subsidiaries of Bank Holding Companies Engaged in Underwriting and Dealing in Securities,* Docket

No. R-0841, March 6, 1997.

11. Adam Nguyen and Matt Watkins, "Recent Legislation: Financial Services Reform," *President and Fellows of Harvard College, Harvard Journal on Legislation*, Summer 2000.

12. Paul J. Polking and Scott A. Cammarn, "Overview of Gramm-Leach-Bliley Act," *University of North Carolina School of Law Banking Institute, North Carolina Banking Institute,* April 2000.

13. Adam Nguyen and Matt Watkins, "Recent Legislation: Financial Services Reform," *President and Fellows of Harvard College, Harvard Journal on Legislation*, Summer 2000.

14. Jonathan R Macey, "The Business of Banking Before and After Gramm-Leach-Bliley," *University of Iowa, the Journal of Corporation Law, Vol. 25,* Summer 2000.

15. ibid.

16. Congressional Research Service, The Library of Congress, *Fannie Mae and Freddie Mac in Conservatorship,* September 15, 2008.

17. United States Government Accountability Office, Testimony Before the U.S. Senate Committee on Banking, Housing, and Urban Affairs, *Troubled Asset Relief Program, Status of Efforts to Address Transparency and Accountability Issues*, September 24, 2009.

18. Fox Business Network, *BofA to Get $20B More From TARP, Plus Backstop on $118B,* http://www.foxbusiness.com/story/markets/industries/finance/bofa-shares-falter-reports-needs-new-tarp-money/#.

19. Morning Star, Inc, Historical Stock Quotes, November 15, 2009, http://quicktake.morningstar.com/stocknet/Price1.aspx?Country=USA&Symbol=BSC.

20. New York Times, Lehman Brothers Holdings Inc. News, April 18, 2009, http://topics.nytimes.com/topics/news/business/companies/lehman_brothers_holdings_inc.

21. American International Group, Our Commitment, *The AIG Financial Crisis: A Summary,* May 1, 2009,

http://www.aig.com/Our_Comitment_385_136429.html.
22. ibid.
23. Citi Group, Annual Report 2007.
24. Citi Group, Annual Report 2008.
25. U.S. Treasury Department, Office of Financial Stability, *Troubled Asset Relief Program Transactions Report*, November 4, 2009.
26. Citi Group, *Interim Report, 3rd Quarter 2009*, October 15, 2009.
27. Merrill Lynch & Co. Inc., Annual Report 2008.
28. Merrill Lynch & Co. Inc., *Press Release: Bank of America Buys Merrill Lynch* September 15,2008; *Creating Unique Financial Services Firm,* September 15,2008.
29. Congressional Research Service, *Hedge Funds: Should They Be Regulated?* July 13, 2009.
30. U.S. Securities and Exchange Commission, *Hedging Your Bets: A Heads Up on Hedge Funds and Funds of Hedge Funds*, May 25, 2009.
31. U.S. Department of Treasury, The President's Working Group on Financial Markets, *Hedge Funds, Leverage and the Lessons of Long Term Capital Management,* April 1999.
32. Louise Story, "Investors Flee as Hedge Fund Woes Deepen," *New York Times,* October 23, 2008.
33. U.S. Department of Treasury, *Financial Regulatory Reform—A New Foundation: Rebuilding Financial Supervision and Regulation,* 2009.
34. American Bankers Association and Edward L. Yingling, "Proposal for Financial Regulatory Reform," Testimony before the Committee on Financial Services, United States House of Representatives, July 15, 2009, http://www.aba.com/pressroom/071509HFSCRegReform.htm.
35. Office of Thrift Supervision, *About the OTS: History*. March 29, 2009, http://www.ots.gov/?p=History.
36. American Bankers Association and Edward L. Yingling, "Proposal for Financial Regulatory Reform," Testimony before the Committee on Financial Services, United States House of Representatives, July 15, 2009, http://www.aba.com/pressroom/071509HFSCRegReform.htm.

www.ingramcontent.com/pod-product-compliance
Lightning Source LLC
Chambersburg PA
CBHW051420280526
45785CB00003B/1098